Good Question!

Which Way to Freedom?
AND OTHER QUESTIONS ABOUT . . .
the Underground Railroad

STERLING CHILDREN'S BOOKS
New York

STERLING CHILDREN'S BOOKS

New York

An Imprint of Sterling Publishing
387 Park Avenue South
New York, NY 10016

Photo Credits: 10 top left & bottom center: Library of Congress; 10 top center: Rare Books Department/Boston Public Library; 10 top right & bottom left: private collection; 10 bottom right: Courtesy of Bibliothèque et Archives Nationales du Québec; 17: Brooklyn Museum of Art/Courtesy Wikimedia Foundation; 22 left: National Portrait Gallery; 22 top & bottom right: Library of Congress; 30 top & bottom left: Courtesy Wikimedia Foundation; 30 top right: private collection; 30 bottom right: Library of Congress

ISBN 978-1-4549-0784-8 (hardcover)
ISBN 978-1-4549-0785-5 (paperback)

Distributed in Canada by Sterling Publishing
c/o CanadianManda Group, 165 Dufferin Street
Toronto, Ontario, Canada M6K 3H6
Distributed in the United Kingdom by GMC Distribution Services
Castle Place, 166 High Street, Lewes, East Sussex, England BN7 1XU
Distributed in Australia by Capricorn Link (Australia) Pty. Ltd.
P.O. Box 704, Windsor, NSW 2756, Australia

Design by Andrea Miller
Art by Jim Madsen

For information about custom editions, special sales, and premium and corporate purchases, please contact
Sterling Special Sales at 800-805-5489 or specialsales@sterlingpublishing.com.

Manufactured in China
Lot #:
2 4 6 8 10 9 7 5 3
06/15

www.sterlingpublishing.com/kids

CONTENTS

Why was there slavery in the United States?

When the United States declared independence from England in 1776, slavery was legal in all thirteen colonies. White European settlers wanted cheap labor to turn wilderness into farms and towns. They also wanted laborers who could easily be identified. Buying and enslaving black Africans kidnapped from their homes cost less than paying field hands. Enslaved people weren't paid and couldn't quit. By law they were property, like plows and workhorses. Many wealthy and important Americans, including George Washington, Benjamin Franklin, and Thomas Jefferson, were slaveholders.

Meanwhile, countries around the world were outlawing the enslavement of human beings. The United States finally declared the importation of enslaved people illegal in 1808. Americans could no longer buy newly captured Africans. But people who were already enslaved within the country could still be bought and sold, and any child born to an enslaved mother became the property of her slaveholder.

By 1860, slavery in the United States had changed. All sixteen Northern states prohibited slavery, as did the new states California and Oregon. But it remained legal in the South, where one out of every three people was enslaved. Some four million enslaved people lived in the fifteen Southern states and the District of Columbia, the nation's capital. Most of these men, women, and children lived and worked on large farms that grew crops such as cotton, rice, and tobacco. These plantations were farming factories powered by men and women who picked and planted crops— even children were forced to work. Millions of enslaved people were the machines that made plantations profitable.

Powerful plantation owners kept slavery alive by getting pro-slavery laws passed. Enslaved people were treated like livestock. Their children could be taken and sold like calves or lambs. And when slaveholders died, the enslaved people they held captive became the property of their heirs. Slaveholders used these laws, as well as abuse and punishment, to control enslaved people. Even mailing anti-slavery pamphlets was illegal in the South. So was helping someone escape.

Did enslaved people try to escape?

Plantation life was full of hard work and misery. Men, women, and kids toiled as servants and field hands. They cooked and cleaned, plowed and hoed, picked and pulled for endless hours under the hot summer sun or cold rainy sky. Field hands were constantly watched by overseers. Overseers beat or whipped workers who didn't keep up the pace. Enslaved people couldn't take a break or get water without permission. The job of overseers was to get as much work out of them as possible, day after day.

Living conditions were bad, too. Plantation owners spent as little money as possible on food, clothing, and shelter for enslaved people, who often were given just enough to survive. Most lived on cornmeal and some beans or salt pork. Men got the most food. Mothers had to share their rations with their children. Food was kept locked up, and clothing handed out only once or twice a year. Enslaved people slept in crowded and shoddy shacks or cabins that had dirt floors, leaky roofs, plank walls plastered with mud, fireplaces for cooking and heat, and wooden chimneys that easily caught fire. Nothing belonged to enslaved people—not even their families. Slaveholders in need of money could sell off someone's father or daughter. Enslaved people never knew when their families might be torn apart.

It's easy to imagine wanting to run away. But think about what it was like to be an enslaved plantation worker in the South. It was illegal to teach enslaved people to read or write, so most couldn't read maps and signs or write messages. Most had never been anywhere but the plantation. They knew no other place or anyone who lived elsewhere. Choosing to leave meant never seeing their family again. Enslaved people didn't have money, extra food, or any way to travel except by foot. Where could they go and how could they know how to get there? It wasn't easy to escape, and most runaways were caught.

What was the Underground Railroad?

The Underground Railroad was a secret network that helped enslaved people escape to freedom. It wasn't a bunch of sunken tunnels full of train cars. In fact, it was neither underground nor an actual railroad. That's just what people called it. Why? Things that are underground are hidden and often secret. This network needed to be hidden, too. Helping an enslaved person escape was illegal. Runaways were criminals and fugitives from the law. Their crime was stealing valuable property—themselves! Aiding a runaway was a crime, too. If captured, fugitives and those who helped them could be punished. The runaways might even be killed.

Like any railroad, the Underground Railroad carried passengers from one place to another. It had stations and made stops along the way. But the Underground Railroad wasn't a formal group. There weren't offices or membership cards. It was just people willing to help others along the path to freedom. The Underground Railroad included helpers, safe hiding places, and routes out of slavery. Sometimes it was an organized network. For example, people in a chain of towns who shuttled runaways from place to place in wagons. Other times the Underground Railroad meant someone's cellar where runaways could safely sleep, or a bundle of food left on a porch.

Enslaved people escaped any way they could, and to any place where slavery was illegal. Some went to "free" states in the North. Others made their way to Canada, Mexico, or onto ships going to the Caribbean. It's hard to know exactly how many runaways got help along the way. Some historians estimate that during the 1800s more than one hundred thousand people successfully rode the Underground Railroad to freedom.

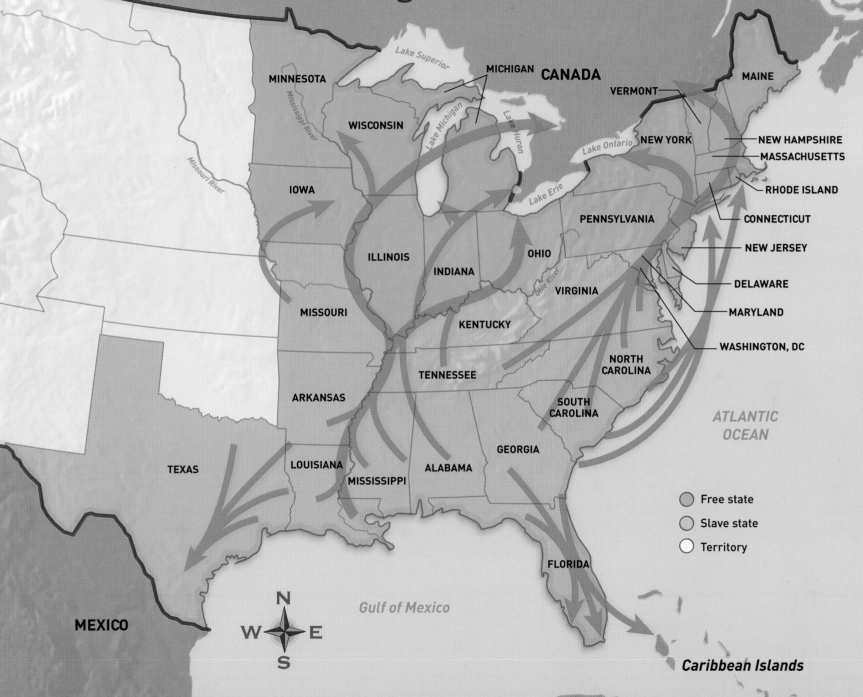

The Underground Railroad

CANADA

MINNESOTA

MICHIGAN

Lake Superior

WISCONSIN

Lake Michigan

Lake Huron

IOWA

MAINE

VERMONT

NEW YORK

Lake Ontario

NEW HAMPSHIRE

MASSACHUSETTS

RHODE ISLAND

Lake Erie

PENNSYLVANIA

CONNECTICUT

ILLINOIS

INDIANA

OHIO

NEW JERSEY

Mississippi River

Missouri River

MISSOURI

KENTUCKY

VIRGINIA

Ohio River

DELAWARE

MARYLAND

WASHINGTON, DC

ARKANSAS

TENNESSEE

NORTH
CAROLINA

SOUTH
CAROLINA

TEXAS

LOUISIANA

MISSISSIPPI

ALABAMA

GEORGIA

MEXICO

Gulf of Mexico

FLORIDA

ATLANTIC
OCEAN

N
W E
S

Caribbean Islands

Free state

Slave state

Territory

LEVI COFFIN

Levi Coffin and his wife, Catherine, were abolitionists who helped fugitives move across Indiana and Ohio.

THOMAS GARRETT

Thomas Garrett housed and aided runaways near Philadelphia as well as in the Maryland and Delaware border region.

WILLIAM STILL

William Still documented the experiences of runaways. He and his wife, Letitia, gave shelter to hundreds of fugitives escaping slavery.

SOLOMON NORTHUP

Solomon Northup wrote a book about his life, called *Twelve Years A Slave*. It was popular during his lifetime and has been made into movies.

HARRIET TUBMAN

Harriet Tubman led enslaved people to freedom as an Underground Railroad conductor, and she fought in the Civil War.

ALEXANDER MILTON ROSS

Alexander Milton Ross was known as "Birdman" to Underground Railroad workers. He helped enslaved people escape while he pretended to be just a bird watcher.

Who worked on the Underground Railroad, and why?

Most Underground Railroad workers were other African Americans. Runaways who had successfully escaped and those still enslaved helped thousands of fugitives reach freedom. Free black people helped, too. These were men and women who had been born free or had somehow gained their freedom. It's easy to understand why so many African Americans took part in the work of the Underground Railroad. Many knew firsthand the conditions fugitives were running from. Others had family members they hoped to help. Runaways often found other black people easier to trust than white strangers—especially in the South, where slavery was legal. Nobody knows how many people helped runaways to freedom. The Underground Railroad was secret, and many who knew its stories died without telling them.

Abolitionists were people who wanted to abolish, or end, slavery. They believed slavery was cruel, wrong, and bad for the United States. Some white abolitionists helped runaways escape. Many were members of religious groups, like the Quakers, that believed slavery was a sin against God. Levi Coffin and Thomas Garrett were two famous Quakers who worked on the Underground Railroad. They helped thousands of fugitives escape. As Coffin explained, "The Bible, in bidding us to feed the hungry and clothe the naked, said nothing about color."

Who was the father of the Underground Railroad?

William Still was a black man who was born free in the state of New Jersey. His mother had escaped slavery in Maryland, and his father had purchased his own freedom. As a young man, Still moved to Philadelphia, where he worked as a clerk for the Pennsylvania Anti-Slavery Society. In 1872, Still published the first written history of the Underground Railroad. "These facts must never be lost sight of," he wrote. He believed that the stories would inspire

What was a conductor?

Guiding fugitives to safety was the risky job of an Underground Railroad "conductor." Conductors took runaways from one place to the next on their journey to freedom. Sometimes this meant walking with them through the night, hiding runaways from lawmen, and fighting off people trying to catch fugitives. Conductors might also shuttle runaways in horse-drawn wagons. Fugitives hid under straw or in secret compartments underneath fake wagon floors. Boats were also used to transport runaways. The Ohio River was the border between the slave states of Kentucky and Virginia and the free states of Illinois, Indiana, and Ohio. Thousands crossed this river as they fled north.

In the mid 1800s, Ripley, Ohio, was a bustling riverside town across the Ohio River from northeastern Kentucky. It was also a hub of abolition activity—the perfect home for Underground Railroad conductor John Parker. Parker was born into slavery in Virginia. At age eight he was taken from his mother, sold, and marched in chains all the way to Alabama. Parker tried to escape a number of times, but he was always caught. Eventually Parker convinced a widow to buy him as an investment. He was a skilled ironworker and promised to make her a lot of money. Slaveholders could hire out enslaved people to make money. Some were allowed to keep a fraction of their earnings. In rare cases, enslaved people could use this money to purchase themselves and be declared free. This was how Parker managed to save $1,800 and buy his freedom.

Parker lived in Ripley to help others become free. At night, he would take his boat across the river to the Kentucky side. "Every night of the year saw runaways . . . making their way stealthily to the country north," Parker wrote. He rowed the fugitives that he found to Ripley. From there he put them on the path northward. Parker worked with other Underground Railroad workers, including the Rankin family. Reverend John Rankin lit a lantern in his window to let runaways on the Kentucky side know it was safe to cross the river.

What were stations and who were stationmasters?

Underground Railroad stations were safe houses—places where fugitives could find shelter. An Underground Railroad station might just be an unlocked farm cellar where a runaway could sleep safely. Perhaps there would be a plate of food, too. Other stations were more full-service. Some of the people who ran the safe houses, the stationmasters, fed and clothed whole families of runaways and gave advice on where to go next. Many Underground Railroad workers were stationmasters. William Still's home was among many famous Underground Railroad stations in Philadelphia. Thomas Garrett's family hid runaways at their farm when he was a child. Garrett did the same at his own home in Delaware. Reverend John Rankin's home was one in a chain of safe houses that conductors shuttled runaways to as they made their way north through Ohio. There were stations with hidden rooms behind bookcases, and trapdoors under rugs. These secret rooms were used for hiding when lawmen came looking. Towns like Springboro, Ohio, that were built by Quakers, even had tunnels that connected homes.

Did stationmasters send secret messages?

Underground Railroad workers had to use secret codes and signals to safely pass along information. To safely identify themselves, runaways might be told to make a bird call or use a secret knock. Stationmasters let fugitives know it was safe with lit lanterns, scarves tied on gates, or quilts on clotheslines. Sometimes workers needed to send a stationmaster a written message in code. Only Underground Railroad workers knew that "ten packages arriving Friday, three of them small," meant "expect ten runaways, three of them children."

June 9, 1859

Forwarding a load of potatoes on the Freedom train. Expect ten packages Friday, three of them small.

UNDERGROUND RAILROAD CODE WORDS

UNDERGROUND RAILROAD AGENT: Someone who made arrangements and planned routes for escaping runaways.

BAGGAGE, PARCEL, PACKAGE, CARGO, SHIPMENT, PASSENGER, TRAVELER: Escaping fugitives or runaways.

BRAKEMAN: Someone in the free states or Canada who helped new arrivals settle in.

CONDUCTOR or SHEPHERD: A person who guided runaways to safe places.

FORWARDING: Moving fugitives from station to station.

FREEDOM TRAIN: The Underground Railroad.

HEAVEN: Canada.

LOAD OF POTATOES: A wagonload of runaways hidden under hay or potatoes.

STATION: A safe house where fugitives were sheltered.

STATIONMASTER: A person who ran a safe house.

STOCKHOLDER: Someone who donated money, clothing, or food to the Underground Railroad.

"THE WIND BLOWS FROM THE SOUTH TODAY": An alert to Underground Railroad workers that runaways were in the area.

"THE TRAIN IS OFF THE TRACK": There's trouble in transporting the runaways.

"IT'S A FRIEND WITH FRIENDS": Code words used by a conductor arriving at a safe house with a group of fugitives.

"LOST A PASSENGER": A runaway was captured.

Which way to freedom?

It wasn't easy for an enslaved person to figure out how to escape and where to go. Information about safe traveling routes or where to find help was hard to come by. Those who ran away often just disappeared. No one knew how they'd escaped or even if they had made it out successfully. Enslaved people might talk among themselves about escape routes they'd heard of, but there was no way to know if the information was true—or if it could be trusted. Asking questions could get you in trouble. Slaveholders and overseers might have spies—enslaved people tempted to betray secrets for extra food, an easier job, or to avoid punishment.

Some Underground Railroad workers, called agents, spread information in creative and sly ways about safe routes and willing helpers. Agents would visit plantations, pretending to be traveling doctors, ministers, salespeople, or even fruit pickers. Once there, they'd try to gain the trust of enslaved people. The agents would then pass information on to them about where to cross rivers, and whom they could seek out for help in different towns. Underground Railroad agent Alexander Ross was a doctor and a bird-watcher. He'd visit plantations, telling the owners he wanted to look for birds on their property. When Ross met enslaved people who wanted to run away, he'd give them a compass and instructions on where to go.

The most heavily traveled routes of the Underground Railroad ran through Maryland, Delaware, and Kentucky in the South, and Ohio, Indiana, and Pennsylvania in the North. Cities like Washington, DC, Baltimore, Philadelphia, and New York were major hubs on the Underground Railroad. Before the mid-1800s, runaways often settled in cities in the North. Many of these cities were known havens for escaped fugitives with welcoming communities of free black people. But harsher laws passed in 1850 meant black people were no longer safe from fugitive hunters, even in the free northern states. Because of the new law, many set off for Canada, where slavery was illegal everywhere.

Eastman Johnson's famous painting of escaping runaways, *A Ride for Liberty—Fugitive Slaves.*

Were runaways safe in the North?

Even though slavery was illegal in the North, runaways weren't safe there. Southern slaveholders could legally take runaways back. Fugitive hunters tracked down runaways for a bounty, or reward, offered by slaveholders. Sometimes bounty hunters simply sold captured runaways down South. Even free black people could be kidnapped and sold into slavery. Proving that you were a free person could be difficult. Solomon Northup's autobiography, *Twelve Years A Slave*, tells his story of being a free black man in New York who was kidnapped and sold into slavery in Louisiana. Northup spent a dozen years away from his family before regaining his freedom.

The North became less and less safe for runaways as time went on. Once the Fugitive Slave Act passed in 1850, things got worse. The new law made it the federal government's job to capture and return runaways. That meant federal marshals could force local lawmen in free states to help them round up suspected runaways. Captured fugitives weren't allowed trials. Slaveholders claiming that a person was their property was proof enough. Abolitionists called the Fugitive Slave Act the "Bloodhound Law," after the dogs used to track down fugitives. The 1850 law also made helping fugitives a more serious federal crime. U.S. marshals could legally search anyone's home to look for runaways and arrest anyone helping fugitives.

The British Empire, including all of Canada, abolished slavery in 1834. After 1850, Canada became the only safe northern destination for fugitives seeking freedom. Canada didn't accept the idea that slaveholders had the right to get runaways back. Runaways in Canada couldn't be forced to return to slavery, unlike those in the northern United States. Many runaways who had lived for years in places like Boston and Philadelphia left for Canada, too. The United States was no longer safe for them.

What was travel like on the journey to freedom?

Even with help, travel on the Underground Railroad was rough and risky. Many brave runaways spent months walking hundreds of miles to reach freedom. It was common for runaways to leave in spring. This gave them the most time to reach the North before winter. Roads and well-traveled paths were easy pickings for bounty hunters. Fugitives instead trudged through thick woods and swampy valleys at night, using the North Star to find their way. Most had little to eat and often slept outdoors. Some stowed away on ships leaving New Orleans, Louisiana, or Mobile, Alabama, for ports in the North. Boats also carried many runaways over one of the Great Lakes to Canada.

Bad weather, getting lost, and going hungry weren't the only dangers. The biggest danger was getting caught. All kinds of people hunted runaways—bounty hunters, lawmen, angry slaveholders, and even crafty con artists. A person might claim to be an Underground Railroad worker but then turn in the runaway for the reward.

Many fugitives avoided capture by disguising themselves. Runaways might carry tools to pass as traveling laborers. Women covered their faces with veils and large bonnets or wore men's clothing. Ellen Craft escaped Georgia by disguising herself as an injured white man. She wore tinted glasses and covered much of her face with a bandage. Her husband, William, posed as her servant!

Who was Henry "Box" Brown?

Henry Brown was enslaved and forced to work in a tobacco factory in Richmond, Virginia. In 1848 his pregnant wife and their three children were sold and sent to North Carolina. Desperate to escape, Brown convinced an abolitionist shoemaker to mail him in a box to Philadelphia. Twenty-seven hours later, the wooden crate arrived at the Pennsylvania Anti-Slavery Society. "When they heard that I was alive," wrote Brown, "they soon managed to break open the box . . . I rose a free-man." He became a famous abolitionist speaker.

After the Civil War, Harriet Tubman settled in Auburn, New York, where she helped raise money for the education of formerly enslaved people. She also opened the Harriet Tubman Home for the Aged. Tubman lived to be ninety years old.

Harriet Tubman became an anti-slavery speaker at abolition meetings. Sometimes she was introduced as "Harriet Garrison" to protect her from bounty hunters looking for fugitives.

During the Civil War, Harriet Tubman became the first American woman ever to lead an armed raid into enemy territory.

Who was Harriet Tubman?

Harriet Tubman was born into slavery. Her family was the property of a Maryland plantation owner. After two of her sisters were sold and taken away in chains, their cries filled Tubman's nightmares. When Tubman was in her late twenties, a man from Georgia came to town to buy slaves. Tubman suspected she'd be sold, which meant she would never see her family again. So she ran, escaping alone and on foot through Delaware to the free state of Pennsylvania.

Tubman settled in Philadelphia and found work. She was free, but not happy. How could she be? Her family was still enslaved in Maryland. Tubman vowed to help them escape north. And she did. First she led one of her sisters' families to freedom, then one of her brothers and some friends, her elderly parents, and many groups of strangers. Tubman put her own life at risk by returning to the South at least thirteen times. She refused to let her passengers turn back. Tubman was known to pull a gun on fugitives who wanted to give up the journey. "Dead [men] tell no tales," Tubman would say. "You go on, or die."

For over a decade or so, the famous Underground Railroad conductor led more than seventy people out of slavery. She became known as Moses and claimed, "I never run my train off the track and I never lost a passenger." Harriet Tubman was both fearless and sly. She fooled people hunting fugitives by acting like a helpless old lady. Few suspected that she was helping so many people escape slavery. She was never caught, and once the Civil War began, Tubman used her skills as a scout and spy for the Union Army.

Did Underground Railroad workers get in trouble?

Anyone aiding a fugitive was considered a criminal. That included stationmasters, conductors, and other workers on the Underground Railroad. Punishment depended on the color of your skin and where you were caught. In the North, people convicted of helping runaways had to pay large fines and repay slaveholders for their stolen property. Stationmaster Thomas Garrett lost his business to debt because of fines. But he was unapologetic, saying, "I haven't a dollar in the world, but if thee knows a fugitive who needs a breakfast, send him to me." Punishment was stiffer in the South. Anyone aiding a fugitive could be convicted of kidnapping and theft of human property and could end up in prison for many years. Samuel Smith was the shoemaker who helped nail Henry "Box" Brown into his crate. Smith later got caught shipping other fugitives and spent seven years in prison for it. Underground Railroad workers caught giving runaways weapons could be executed.

But punishments handed out to those aiding runaways were nothing compared to what happened to fugitives if they were captured. These "troublemakers" could expect to be "sold downriver," meaning they were sold to huge plantations in the Deep South, where conditions were harsher and enslaved people were said to be worked to death. Just as they could with a horse or a house, slaveholders could do whatever they wished with their human property, too. They had the law on their side. It clearly stated that enslaved people were property. Slaveholders could even kill enslaved people; it was the usual punishment in many places for trying to run away. Plantation owners and overseers wanted to make examples of runaways, so they whipped, branded, beat, and even hanged runaways.

What was life like with freedom?

By the time fugitives got to their final stop on the Underground Railroad, most were penniless, hungry, worn out, and perhaps injured or ill. Underground Railroad workers called brakemen helped these runaways settle into freedom. Brakemen found jobs and places to live for newly delivered passengers. Runaways who chose to stay in free states like New York and Pennsylvania often joined free black communities. There was safety in numbers and safety in vigilance committees, too. These were groups of people who watched out for bounty hunters or lawmen looking for fugitives. Life was still difficult. Free black people were not citizens and faced terrible discrimination. Stores, churches, and restaurants turned them away. Many streetcars were for white people only, and African-American kids weren't allowed to attend school with white children.

Canada was different. Black people could be citizens, vote, own property, and testify in a court of law. It was safer, too. Runaways weren't considered fugitives in Canada. The U.S. government asked Canada to help return escaped runaways. Canada said no. Any human being on its soil was free. The Underground Railroad code word for Canada said it all—"heaven."

Most people settled in Canadian cities near the border with Michigan and just across the Great Lakes from New York. By the mid-1850s, thousands of runaways lived in Canadian communities like Chatham, Buxton, St. Catharines, and Toronto. They bought land, built homes, joined churches, and started schools. Elgin was a community built in Canada by formerly enslaved people. Its school was known as the best in the county, and European immigrants sent their children there, too. These new Canadians worked at whatever jobs they could find. Many started out as farmhands and workers, but later owned their own farms and businesses. Mary Ann Shadd Cary was a free black woman who moved to Canada after the Fugitive Slave Law was passed. She started the *Provincial Freeman*, a newspaper that encouraged other free black people as well as fugitives to come to Canada. News of the good life in Canada spread, inspiring others to escape. Supporters of slavery had been claiming that enslaved people could never be independent. The reports from Canada proved them wrong.

What started the Civil War?

The busiest years of the Underground Railroad were those leading up to the Civil War. The nation was growing bigger—and growing apart. Each new state upset the balance between North and South. The U.S. struggled in the 1850s to equalize the power of free and slave states. Underground Railroad activities, autobiographies of escaped runaways, and anti-slavery lectures helped spread the idea of abolitionism. Abraham Lincoln doubted the nation could continue with so much conflict. "A house divided against itself cannot stand," he said. As a presidential candidate, Lincoln pledged to keep slavery out of the new territories—and he won. Within weeks of his election, states in the South seceded. They left the nation, or Union, and in early 1861 started their own country. They called it the Confederate States of America and had their own army. The Civil War had begun.

When did the Underground Railroad stop running?

The Underground Railroad didn't stop when the war began. Agents, conductors, stationmasters, and brakemen continued to help those fleeing slavery. Some enlisted in the Union military. Once African-Americans were allowed to fight, more than two hundred thousand served. In 1863, Lincoln signed the Emancipation Proclamation, declaring enslaved people free in the Confederate states. But it wasn't until Union soldiers took back a Confederate state that anyone was freed. Thousands of enslaved people fled, seeking refuge behind Union battle lines. Stationmasters, agents, and others were there to help feed and shelter the runaways. They also continued to help runaways from Border States escape. The Emancipation Proclamation freed people in Confederate states, but Delaware, Kentucky, Maryland, and Missouri were slave states that had stayed with the Union. Enslaved people in those states remained captive and most weren't free until the Civil War ended and the Thirteenth Amendment passed in 1865. It reads, "Neither slavery nor involuntary servitude . . . shall exist within the United States." That was the day the Underground Railroad stopped running.

From Fugitive to Freedom Fighter

Many people who escaped slavery spent their lives helping
other African-Americans gain their freedom and civil rights.

FREDERICK DOUGLASS

Frederick Douglass fled slavery in Maryland as a
young man. He worked in the anti-slavery movement
and later for the rights of African-Americans.

HENRY BIBB

Henry Bibb ran away from a Kentucky plantation,
eventually settling in Canada, where he started a
newspaper called *Voice of the Fugitive*.

SOJOURNER TRUTH

Sojourner Truth was a famous abolitionist
who gave speeches telling of her own painful
experiences while enslaved. Her words
convinced others that slavery was wrong.

ROBERT SMALLS

Robert Smalls escaped by piloting a Confederate
boat through Charleston harbor and over to the
Union side during the Civil War. He went on to
serve as a U.S. congressman.

Does slavery still exist?

The Thirteenth Amendment abolished all slavery in the United States in 1865. By then slavery was already illegal in Europe and Canada. The few remaining places in South America and the Caribbean where slavery was still legal soon followed. Some of the last nations to outlaw slavery were in the Middle East and North Africa. The Saharan desert country of Mauritania didn't abolish slavery until 1981. Today the enslaving of any human being is illegal everywhere. Slavery is a crime worldwide. But slavery exists in the twenty-first century. Moms and sons, dads and daughters are still being bought and sold like property. An estimated thirty million men, women, and children across the planet are enslaved. Half live in India. Modern slavery is often called human trafficking.

Enslaved people today have many faces. Some are children forced to work or beg for money that goes to their owners. Others are young girls made to marry men and become family servants. Workers are sometimes tricked into slavery by con artists and "coyotes," people who smuggle workers across borders. Sometimes people may think they're being hired for jobs overseas, but when they arrive, they're forced to work without being paid. In parts of South Asia and West Africa, some babies are born into slavery still. Some cultures have local traditions that view certain groups or classes of people as enslaved from birth.

Like long-ago workers on the Underground Railroad, compassionate people are still helping enslaved people find freedom. Today's freedom fighters have something previous generations didn't—the law is on their side. International organizations and governments are working to stop human trafficking. Freedom is a human right that belongs to all people.